Continuing Innovation
IN INFORMATION TECHNOLOGY

Committee on Depicting Innovation in Information Technology

Computer Science and Telecommunications Board

Division on Engineering and Physical Sciences

NATIONAL RESEARCH COUNCIL
OF THE NATIONAL ACADEMIES

THE NATIONAL ACADEMIES PRESS
Washington, D.C.
www.nap.edu

THE NATIONAL ACADEMIES PRESS   500 Fifth Street, NW   Washington, DC 20001

NOTICE: The project that is the subject of this report was approved by the Governing Board of the National Research Council, whose members are drawn from the councils of the National Academy of Sciences, the National Academy of Engineering, and the Institute of Medicine. The members of the committee responsible for the report were chosen for their special competences and with regard for appropriate balance.

Support for this project was provided by the National Science Foundation under sponsor award number IIS-0840364. Any opinions expressed in this material are those of the authors and do not necessarily reflect the views of the agencies and organizations that provided support for the project.

Figure 1 designed by Dmitry Krasny, Deka Design. Text layout by Estelle Miller, The National Academies Press.

International Standard Book Number-13: 978-0-309-25962-0
International Standard Book Number-10: 0-309-25962-2

Copies of this report are available from

The National Academies Press
500 Fifth Street, NW, Keck 360
Washington, DC 20001
800/624-6242
202/334-3313
http://www.nap.edu

Copyright 2012 by the National Academy of Sciences. All rights reserved.

Printed in the United States of America

THE NATIONAL ACADEMIES
Advisers to the Nation on Science, Engineering, and Medicine

The **National Academy of Sciences** is a private, nonprofit, self-perpetuating society of distinguished scholars engaged in scientific and engineering research, dedicated to the furtherance of science and technology and to their use for the general welfare. Upon the authority of the charter granted to it by the Congress in 1863, the Academy has a mandate that requires it to advise the federal government on scientific and technical matters. Dr. Ralph J. Cicerone is president of the National Academy of Sciences.

The **National Academy of Engineering** was established in 1964, under the charter of the National Academy of Sciences, as a parallel organization of outstanding engineers. It is autonomous in its administration and in the selection of its members, sharing with the National Academy of Sciences the responsibility for advising the federal government. The National Academy of Engineering also sponsors engineering programs aimed at meeting national needs, encourages education and research, and recognizes the superior achievements of engineers. Dr. Charles M. Vest is president of the National Academy of Engineering.

The **Institute of Medicine** was established in 1970 by the National Academy of Sciences to secure the services of eminent members of appropriate professions in the examination of policy matters pertaining to the health of the public. The Institute acts under the responsibility given to the National Academy of Sciences by its congressional charter to be an adviser to the federal government and, upon its own initiative, to identify issues of medical care, research, and education. Dr. Harvey V. Fineberg is president of the Institute of Medicine.

The **National Research Council** was organized by the National Academy of Sciences in 1916 to associate the broad community of science and technology with the Academy's purposes of furthering knowledge and advising the federal government. Functioning in accordance with general policies determined by the Academy, the Council has become the principal operating agency of both the National Academy of Sciences and the National Academy of Engineering in providing services to the government, the public, and the scientific and engineering communities. The Council is administered jointly by both Academies and the Institute of Medicine. Dr. Ralph J. Cicerone and Dr. Charles M. Vest are chair and vice chair, respectively, of the National Research Council.

www.national-academies.org

COMMITTEE ON DEPICTING INNOVATION IN INFORMATION TECHNOLOGY

PETER LEE, Microsoft Research, *Chair*
MARK E. DEAN, IBM Corporation
DEBORAH L. ESTRIN, University of California, Los Angeles
JAMES T. KAJIYA, Microsoft Corporation
PRABHAKAR RAGHAVAN, Google, Inc.
ANDREW J. VITERBI, Viterbi Group, LLC

Staff

JON K. EISENBERG, CSTB Director
EMILY ANN MEYER, Study Director
SHENAE BRADLEY, Senior Program Assistant

COMPUTER SCIENCE AND TELECOMMUNICATIONS BOARD

ROBERT F. SPROULL, Oracle (retired), *Chair*
PRITHVIRAJ BANERJEE, Hewlett Packard Company
STEVEN M. BELLOVIN, Columbia University
JACK L. GOLDSMITH III, Harvard Law School
SEYMOUR E. GOODMAN, Georgia Institute of Technology
JON M. KLEINBERG, Cornell University
ROBERT KRAUT, Carnegie Mellon University
SUSAN LANDAU, Harvard University
PETER LEE, Microsoft Research
DAVID LIDDLE, U.S. Venture Partners
DAVID E. SHAW, D.E. Shaw Research
ALFRED Z. SPECTOR, Google, Inc.
JOHN STANKOVIC, University of Virginia
JOHN SWAINSON, Dell, Inc.
PETER SZOLOVITS, Massachusetts Institute of Technology
PETER J. WEINBERGER, Google, Inc.
ERNEST J. WILSON, University of Southern California
KATHERINE YELICK, University of California, Berkeley

Staff

JON K. EISENBERG, Director
RENEE HAWKINS, Financial and Administrative Manager
HERBERT S. LIN, Chief Scientist
LYNETTE I. MILLETT, Senior Program Officer
EMILY ANN MEYER, Program Officer
VIRGINIA BACON TALATI, Associate Program Officer
ENITA A. WILLIAMS, Associate Program Officer
SHENAE BRADLEY, Senior Program Assistant
ERIC WHITAKER, Senior Program Assistant

Preface

In 1995, the National Research Council's (NRC's) Computer Science and Telecommunications Board (CSTB) produced the report *Evolving the High Performance Computing and Communications Initiative to Support the Nation's Information Infrastructure*.[1] A graphic in that report, often called the "tire tracks" diagram because of its appearance, produced an extraordinary response by clearly linking investments in academic and industry research to the ultimate creation of new information technology (IT) industries with more than $1 billion in annual revenue.[2] Used in presentations to Congress and executive branch decision makers and discussed broadly in the research and innovation policy communities, the tire tracks figure dispelled the assumption that the commercially successful IT industry is self-sufficient, underscoring how much industry instead builds on government-funded university research, sometimes through long incubation periods of years and even decades. It also compellingly illustrates the complex nature of research in the field and the interdependencies between various subfields of computing and communications research.

The figure was updated in the 2002 CSTB report *Information Technology Research, Innovation, and E-Government* and again in the 2003 CSTB report *Innovation in Information Technology*, largely through the addition of tracks in important new areas such as entertainment and data mining. The 2003 report also distilled key lessons from eight prior CSTB studies about the nature of research in information technology—including the unpredictability of and synergy among research results; the roles of government, industry, and academia; and the social returns from research. A 2009 report, *Assessing the Impacts of Changes in the Information Technology R&D Ecosystem: Retaining Leadership in an Increasingly Global Environment*, reproduced the 2003 update to the diagram and explored many of the related themes.

Computing research and its impacts have continued to evolve and blossom in the years since the 2003 version of the tire tracks figure was published. With the support of the National Science

---

[1] All NRC/CSTB reports referred to in this preface were published by the National Academy Press/The National Academies Press, Washington, D.C., in the year indicated.

[2] IT advances have of course also had profound impacts on nearly every major industry sector, not just IT industries; these indirect effects were not the focus of the present project.

> **Statement of Task**
>
> A small committee will update a previously issued figure depicting the role that government-supported, academic, and industrial research plays in the formation of major new IT capabilities (as measured by the emergence of billion-dollar information technology industries). The update will introduce additional billion-dollar industries and other developments as appropriate. A brief report will highlight the updated tire tracks figure and summarize key points from past CSTB reports related to the results of IT research; the nature and success of the U.S. research partnership among government, industry, and universities; economic payoffs of investments in research; and the evolution of the U.S. IT R&D ecosystem. The report will not contain any new findings and recommendations.

Foundation, CSTB undertook a project to prepare an update. The task of the Committee on Depicting Innovation in Information Technology was threefold (see box): (1) to reconsider important research areas and significant billion-dollar-plus IT industries that had emerged since the 2003 report, (2) to reconsider how best to characterize and depict these investments and impacts, and (3) to recap and update the material in the 2003 report that accompanied the tire tracks figure and that presents related lessons on the impact of research on innovation in information technology.

In updating the content of the figure, the committee drew on the earlier CSTB work as well as the committee's own knowledge of key research contributions and results, and also obtained input on these from a number of computing researchers whose contributions are acknowledged below. The committee conducted meetings by teleconference and collaborated extensively by e-mail to develop the present report. In reconsidering the design of the figure, the committee explored several design approaches, some quite different from that in the original 1995 figure, and worked with a designer to explore alternatives. Ultimately, the committee decided to retain many features of the original tire tracks while somewhat changing the overall structure and adding some elements as outlined in the first section of this report.

The new figure is accompanied by a brief text based in large part on prior CSTB reports. Unless otherwise indicated in the notes, the primary source is the 2003 report *Innovation in Information Technology*. Where appropriate, the committee has updated the text to provide more current information and recent examples. For readability, direct extracts from earlier CSTB work are not set in quotation marks.

The committee thanks the following researchers who provided input on specific technical and research questions: Yossi Azar, Victor Bahl, Suman Banerjee, Doug Burger, Surajit Chaudhuri, Carlos Guestrin, Hauges Hoppe, Andrew Hopper, Eric Horvitz, Butler Lampson, James Landay, Paul Larson, Ed Lazowska, James Lee, David Lomet, Beth Mynatt, David Patterson, Yuval Peres, and Mani Srivastava. We also are sincerely appreciative of the services and leadership of Eugene Spafford, chair of the committee from September 2009 to January 2011. Finally, the committee thanks Dmitry Krasny, Deka Design, for his expert design assistance in realizing the committee's vision for Figure 1.

Peter Lee, *Chair*
Committee on Depicting Innovation in Information Technology

Acknowledgment of Reviewers

This report has been reviewed in draft form by individuals chosen for their diverse perspectives and technical expertise, in accordance with procedures approved by the National Research Council's Report Review Committee. The purpose of this independent review is to provide candid and critical comments that will assist the institution in making its published report as sound as possible and to ensure that the report meets institutional standards for objectivity, evidence, and responsiveness to the study charge. The review comments and draft manuscript remain confidential to protect the integrity of the deliberative process. We wish to thank the following individuals for their review of this report:

Peter Freeman, Georgia Institute of Technology
Susan Graham, University of California, Berkeley
Laura Haas, IBM Almaden Research Center
David Patterson, University of California, Berkeley
Jennifer Rexford, Princeton University
Robert F. Sproull, Oracle (retired)
John Stankovic, University of Virginia
Patrick Winston, Massachusetts Institute of Technology
Katherine Yelick, University of California, Berkeley, and Lawrence Berkeley National Laboratory

Although the reviewers listed above have provided many constructive comments and suggestions, they were not asked to endorse the conclusions or recommendations, nor did they see the final draft of the report before its release. The review of this report was overseen by Joseph Traub, Columbia University. Appointed by the National Research Council, he was responsible for making certain that an independent examination of this report was carried out in accordance with institutional procedures and that all review comments were carefully considered. Responsibility for the final content of this report rests entirely with the authoring committee and the institution.

Contents

The Impact of Information Technology ... 1

Universities, Industry, and Government: A Complex Partnership Yielding Innovation and Leadership ... 2

Key Lessons About the Nature of Research in Information Technology ... 9

Looking Ahead ... 16

Notes ... 18

Appendix A   Short Biographies of Committee Members ... 24

Appendix B   Transfers of Ideas and People and Other Impacts Since 2003 Added to Figure 1 ... 27

Appendix C   Examples of Impacts from Algorithms Research ... 32

The Impact of Information Technology

Information technology (IT) is widely understood to be the enabling technology of the 21st century.[1] IT has transformed, and continues to transform, all aspects of our lives: commerce and finance, education, employment, energy, health care, manufacturing, government, national security, transportation, communications, entertainment, science, and engineering. IT and its impact on the U.S. economy—both directly (the IT sector itself) and indirectly (other sectors that are powered by advances in IT)[2]—continue to grow in size and importance.

In total, according to estimates for 2010 by the Bureau of Economic Analysis, the IT-intensive "information-communications-technology-producing" industries[3] grew by 16.3 percent and contributed nearly 5 percent to the overall U.S. gross domestic product (GDP).[4] A 2011 study by the McKinsey Global Institute found that in 2009 Internet-related activities alone contributed an average of 3.8 percent to the U.S. GDP.[5] (By contrast, the total federal funding in fiscal year 2010 for the networking and IT research and development (R&D) program, which includes most federal support for IT R&D, was approximately $4.3 billion,[6] just under 0.03 percent of GDP.[7]) These substantial contributions to the economy reflect only the direct economic benefits of the IT sector and do not capture the full benefits realized from the application of IT throughout the economy.

To appreciate the magnitude and breadth of its achievements, imagine spending a day without IT. This would be a day without the Internet and all that it enables. A day without diagnostic medical imaging. A day during which automobiles lacked electronic ignition, antilock brakes, and electronic stability control. A day without digital media—without wireless telephones, high-definition televisions, MP3 audio, cable- or Internet-delivered video, computer animation, and video games. A day during which aircraft could not fly, travelers had to navigate without benefit of the Global Positioning System (GPS), weather forecasters had no models, banks and merchants could not transfer funds electronically, and factory automation ceased to function. It would be a day in which the U.S. military lacked precision munitions, did not have the capabilities for network-centric warfare, and did not enjoy technological supremacy. It would be, for most people in the United States and the rest of the developed world, a "day the Earth stood still."

Universities, Industry, and Government: A Complex Partnership Yielding Innovation and Leadership

One measure of the impact of investment in information technology research and development is its contribution to the creation of numerous U.S. firms with annual revenues exceeding $1 billion and of entire new sectors that contribute billions of dollars to the U.S. economy.[8] Many of these firms are household names, and their products and services underpin the digital economy—and indeed the economy more broadly. The combined estimated annual revenue of only the companies listed on Figure 1 is nearly $500 billion (Table 1).

Figure 1, an update of the 1995 "tire tracks" figure[9] and the intermediate 2003 version,[10] illustrates, through examples, how fundamental research in IT, conducted in industry and universities, has led to the introduction of entirely new product categories that ultimately became billion-dollar industries. It reflects a complex research environment in which concurrent advances in multiple subfields—in particular within computer science and engineering but extending into other fields, too, from electrical engineering to psychology—have been mutually reinforcing, stimulating and enabling one another and leading to vibrant, innovative industries exemplified by top-performing U.S. firms.[11] Figure 1 is of necessity incomplete and symbolic in nature; it would be impossible to chart all of the important cumulative contributions of research and their links to today's products, firms, and industries. For example, Google could be thought of as having benefited from at least three research areas—networking, parallel and distributed systems, and databases.

Listed in the bottom row of Figure 1 are areas where major investments in basic research in subfields of computing and communications have had the impacts shown in the upper portions of the figure. Not depicted but equally important is research on the theoretical and algorithmic foundations of computing more broadly (Box 1). The vertical red tracks represent university-based (and largely federally funded) research, and the blue tracks represent industry R&D (some of which is also government funded). The dashed black lines indicate periods following the introduction of significant commercial products resulting from this research, the green lines represent billion-dollar-plus industries (by annual revenue) stemming from this research, and the thick green lines represent achievement of multibillion-dollar markets by some of the industries. The top rows list the present-day IT market segments and representative U.S. firms and products whose creation was stimulated by the decades-long research represented by the red and blue vertical tracks.

FIGURE 1 Examples of the contributions of federally supported fundamental research to the creation of IT sectors, firms, and products with large economic impact. Tracks added since the 2003 update of the figure are described in Appendix B. See also Box 1 and Appendix C.

TABLE 1 Annual Revenue Associated with the IT Industry Sector for Key U.S. IT Firms Listed in Figure 1

Industry	Company and Estimated Revenue ($ Billion)[a]	
Broadband and Mobile	Qualcomm*	11
	Motorola	8.2
Microprocessors	nVidia	3.5
	Intel	54
	AMD	5.0
	Texas Instruments	2.1
Personal Computing	Dell	34
	HP	41
	Apple	89
	Symantec	6.2
Internet and Web	Juniper	4.4
	Cisco	43
	Akamai	1.2
	Twitter (estimated)	0.1
	Facebook	3.7
	eBay	12
	Amazon	25
	Google*	22
	Yahoo!	5.0
Cloud Computing	Google (non-advertising)*	1.1
	VMware*	2.9
	Amazon (non-e-commerce)	1.4
Enterprise Systems	Oracle*	31
	IBM	44
	Microsoft	39
Entertainment and Design	Electronic Arts*	3.6
	Pixar	0.5-1.0
	Adobe	4.2
Robotics and Assistive Technologies	iRobot*	0.4
	Nuance	1.3
	Intuitive Surgical*	1.8

NOTE: Revenues are for FY 2011 except as indicated by an asterisk for firms whose listed revenues are 2010-based.
   [a] Sources for estimated revenue listed are given in the section "Notes" following the main text of this report.

> **BOX 1**
> **Research in the Theoretical and Algorithmic Foundations of Computing**
>
> Are there problems that simply cannot be solved by a computer algorithm? If so, what are they, and why is this so? For the problems that *can* be solved, how efficiently (in terms of time, memory, or communications requirements) can this be done? And for those that can't be solved, can we make practical use of this fact, for example, to help ensure better privacy on our computer systems?
>
> These are some of the most basic questions in computing. Research to address such questions is often motivated by the desire to understand the basic nature of computation rather than to find practical applications. However, time and again discoveries are made that provide new ways to solve difficult algorithmic problems. For example, research in coding theory, which investigates the fundamental limits in the encoding and decoding of messages, has led to methods for transmitting messages in ways that are highly tolerant of faulty communications channels, and ultimately to methods that achieve very close to the maximum possible efficiency and provide a foundation for nearly all of today's wireless technologies, ranging from mobile phones, to WiFi, to deep-space communications.
>
> The impact of theoretical and algorithmic research is wide-ranging. Algorithms for network congestion provide the key building block for today's content-distribution networks. Modern logistics systems, such as those used by the airline industry or package delivery systems, depend on a deep understanding of the limits of computation and algorithms for optimal allocation of resources and for scheduling. All modern search engines make use of fundamental knowledge of how mathematical concepts such as eigenvalues can be used to rank Web pages. All electronic commerce today is built on foundational concepts of so-called one-way functions, developed in some of the most theoretical computing research endeavors. And today's speech and natural language understanding systems apply large-scale statistical analysis algorithms in sophisticated ways.
>
> Additional examples of the impacts from algorithms research are provided in Appendix C.

Although the tracks in Figure 1 were chosen to illustrate through prominent examples how each selected research area is connected with a closely linked industry area, in reality each research area is linked in many ways to one or more industry areas. Research outcomes in one area have continued to affect and enable research in other areas. Furthermore, synergies among research areas often lead to surprising results and have impacts on industry that were not originally intended or envisioned (Table 2). This characteristic of technological innovation is most evident in the broad-based impact of research on basic questions in computing. Such research often starts as a search for fundamental knowledge but time and again produces practical technologies that enable significant economic impact, in areas as diverse as optimal resource allocation and scheduling, compact encodings of signals, efficient search algorithms, fair auction and voting mechanisms, and ultralarge-scale statistical analyses. (Box 1 provides further discussion.)

The arrows between the vertical tracks represent some salient examples of the rich interplay between academic research, industry research, and products and indicate the cross-fertilization resulting from multi-directional flows of ideas, technologies, and people (examples are given in Appendix B). Also illustrated in Figure 1 is how products arising from industry can shape academic research. (For example, Microsoft's Kinect sensor is now being used in many research applications, and Google's practical application of MapReduce introduced new ideas about web-scale distributed computing to the research community.) Arrows spanning research areas provide a few indications of the interdependence of research advances in various areas.

TABLE 2 Original Goals, Unanticipated Results, Current Results, and Possible Future Directions for Research Topics in Figure 1

Research Topic	Original Goal	Unanticipated Results
Digital Communications	Untethered communication	Wireless local area networking for computers, cell phones
Computer Architecture	Tools to manage increasing complexity of microprocessor designs; new architectures to dramatically increase processing power	Powerful computation in things such as cars, televisions, kitchen appliances, and mobile devices
Software Technologies	More effective use of computing power for specific tasks, and the creation of common systems on which to run them	Open-source movement that inspired many to gain powerful technical skills and become entrepreneurs; the ability to create software systems of extraordinary scale and complexity
Networking	Sharing computational resources and data among computers	Network e-mail; widespread sharing of software and data; the interconnection of billions of computers and other devices
Parallel and Distributed Systems	Using multiple computers and/or processors to solve a complex problem	Emergence of businesses such as Google and Amazon that use multiple very large data centers to deliver services at large scale
Databases	Tools for managing, discovering, and locating information	Search engines, digital libraries, and data mining and analytics on massive data sets; advances in databases that have led to the development of enormous data repositories—improving knowledge and supporting new forms of scientific discovery
Computer Graphics	Display of real-time graphics and text on an external screen	Graphical user interfaces; techniques for realistic modeling and simulation applied for near-realistic video games and movies; support by these technologies for applications in training and scientific exploration
Artificial Intelligence and Robotics	Simulation of human-level intelligence, including language understanding, vision, learning, and planning	Robotic-enabled prosthetics and artificial organs; fly-by-wire avionics and antilock brakes; cars capable of parallel parking themselves; intelligent ranking of Web search results

[a]Sources for details listed are given in the section "Notes" following the main text of this report.

Today[a]	Advances Expected with Continued Commitment to IT Research[a]
Wireless and broadband industry. Nearly 6 billion cell phone subscribers worldwide, including more than 320 million subscribers in the United States; 54% of the U.S. population as active mobile-broadband subscribers, and more than 87 million fixed broadband subscriptions	Pervasive/ubiquitous communications and access to data and computing resources; mobile sensors for monitoring environment and health in real time
Microprocessor industry. 8.3 billion microprocessors produced annually and used pervasively; $40 billion in annual revenue	Increased interplay between hardware and software to achieve performance while managing power and providing easy programmability
Personal computing industry. 1.4 billion PCs in use worldwide as of 2010; U.S. smartphone sales expected to be nearly 100 million in 2011	Parallel software to better use parallel hardware; improved tools for processing very large data sets
Internet and Web industries. One-third of the world's population is online, and 45% of those are under the age of 25; more than 18 billion searches were conducted in October 2011 in the United States (across five major search sites); U.S. retail e-commerce sales for the third quarter of 2011 were $48.2 billion and accounted for 4.6% of total sales; worldwide, annual e-commerce sales were almost $8 trillion; banking, trading, and other financial transactions done by means of the Internet	"Internet of things" (virtually every device/object networked); sensors embedded everywhere, enabling dramatic improvements in automation, efficiency, and safety
Cloud computing industry, an emerging and rapidly growing industry sector. Health IT alone expected to spend more than $1 billion on cloud services by 2013; enterprise spending on public cloud computing services expected to expand 139% from 2010 to 2011	Renewal of efforts in parallelism to sustain growth in computing performance; improvements in scalability with reductions in operating costs for very large data centers
Enterprise systems industry. Widespread use of enterprise resource planning software; world's largest civilian database, Walmart's data warehouse, stores more than 583 terabytes of sales and inventory data built on a massively parallel system	Natural language searches, data management to promote energy-efficient computing, cloud-based data analyses in heterogeneous environments, and other large-scale data management systems
Entertainment industry. CGI movie "Toy Story 3" the highest-grossing film of 2010; 12 feature-length computer-generated-imagery animated films released in 2011; modeling and simulation commonplace in manufacturing and engineering; video games using advanced computer simulation techniques	Tying visualization of large data sets to the simulation code, increased use of augmented reality, search based on images; photography becoming computational
Robotics and sensing industries. Automation commonplace in manufacturing and in specialties such as robot-assisted surgery; use of aerial drones for surveillance becoming commonplace; some household robots	Artificial intelligence agents capable of abstraction and generalization beyond their initial programming; "household" robots for more than vacuuming

Consider how research in the leftmost area in Figure 1—digital communications—has propelled the communications revolution that continues to unfold today:

- Code division multiple access, which had origins in World War II anti-jamming technology and later was used in military communications satellites, was developed and commercialized as a new standard for cellular telephony in the 1990s by Qualcomm, a company founded by DARPA-funded university researchers. It uses unique mathematical codes to modulate transmissions, thus allowing multiple users to efficiently share a radio channel and providing relative immunity to interference.
- Research in the 1990s on multiple-input and multiple-output techniques, beginning with closely related university research and followed by research at Bell Laboratories, has been a fundamental enabler of today's wireless communications technologies.
- Research and serious engineering efforts in universities through the 1990s led to the ability to use complementary metal oxide semiconductor technology for radio-frequency signals, a development that made it possible to include WiFi, GPS, and Bluetooth at low cost in small, mobile devices.
- Early academic research into packet switched networks provided an underpinning for the local area networks that connect computers within homes and businesses as well as for the Internet that links the globe.
- A university spin-off company developed and commercialized a practical approach to digital subscriber line (DSL) technology, which made it possible to provide high-speed data networking over public telephone network lines.

A similar list could be constructed for each of the research areas represented in Figure 1. As Figure 1 and Table 2 illustrate, investments started more than four decades ago have been critical enablers of the products and services in use today. They also illustrate how research can yield important results not originally contemplated when a first investment was made. Finally, they describe some of the open questions that researchers pursue today and suggest some of the potential applications that lie ahead provided there is a continued commitment to IT research.

Key Lessons About the Nature of Research in Information Technology

A number of important lessons about the nature of research in information technology—including the unpredictability of and synergy among research results; the roles of government, industry, and academia; and the economic and social returns from research—can be gleaned from Figure 1 and can also be distilled from past CSTB reports (for a summary, see Box 2).

THE ESSENTIAL ROLE OF THE FEDERAL GOVERNMENT

Innovation in IT is made possible by a complex ecosystem encompassing university and industrial research enterprises, emerging start-up and more mature technology companies, those that finance innovative firms, and the regulatory environment and legal frameworks in which innovation takes place.[12] It was within this ecosystem that the enabling technologies for each of the IT industries illustrated in Figure 1 were created. The government role has coevolved with the development of IT industries: its programs and investments have focused on capabilities not ready for commercialization and on the new needs that emerged as commercial capabilities grew, both of which are moving targets.[13] A 2009 CSTB report, which examined the health of this ecosystem and noted the challenges posed to the U.S. position in IT leadership, underscored the critical importance of this federal investment (Box 3).[14]

Most often, the federal investment that contributed to the development of the industries shown at the top of Figure 1 took the form of grants or contracts awarded to university and industry researchers by the Defense Advanced Research Projects Agency (DARPA) and other defense research agencies[15] and/or the National Science Foundation (NSF), with the latter having come to play an increasingly important role in supporting academic IT research. A shifting mix of other funding agencies has also been involved, reflecting changes in the missions of these agencies and their needs for IT.[16] For example, the Department of Energy (DOE), the National Aeronautics and Space Administration (NASA), and the military services have supported high-performance computing, networking, human-computer interaction, software engineering, embedded and real-time systems, and other kinds of research; the National Institutes of Health invests in research in

> **BOX 2**
> **Lessons About the Nature of Research in Information Technology—A Summary**
>
> - *The results of research*
>   —America's international leadership in IT—leadership that is vital to the nation—springs from a deep tradition of research. . . .
>   —The unanticipated results of research are often as important as the anticipated results—for example, electronic mail and instant messaging were by-products of research in the 1960s that was aimed at making it possible to share expensive computing resources among multiple simultaneous interactive users. . . .
>   —The interaction of research ideas multiplies their impact—for example, concurrent research programs targeted at integrated circuit design, computer graphics, networking, and workstation-based computing strongly reinforced and amplified one another. . . .
>
> - *Research as a partnership*
>   —The success of the IT research enterprise reflects a complex partnership among government, industry, and universities. . . .
>   —The federal government has had and will continue to have an essential role in sponsoring fundamental research in IT—largely university-based—because it does what industry does not and cannot do. . . . Industrial and governmental investments in research reflect different motivations, resulting in differences in style, focus, and time horizon. . . .
>   —Companies have little incentive to invest significantly in activities whose benefits will spread quickly to their rivals. . . . Fundamental research often falls into this category. By contrast, the vast majority of corporate research and development (R&D) addresses product and process development. . . .
>   —Government funding for research has leveraged the effective decision making of visionary program managers and program office directors from the research community, empowering them to take risks in designing programs and selecting grantees. . . . Government sponsorship of research especially in universities also helps to develop the IT talent used by industry, universities, and other parts of the economy. . . .
>
> - *The economic payoff of research*
>   —Past returns on federal investments in IT research have been extraordinary for both U.S. society and the U.S. economy. . . . The transformative effects of IT grow as innovations build on one another and as user know-how compounds. Priming that pump for tomorrow is today's challenge.
>   —When companies create products using the ideas and workforce that result from federally sponsored research, they repay the nation in jobs, tax revenues, productivity increases, and world leadership. . . .
>
> SOURCE: Reprinted from NRC/CSTB, 2009, *Assessing the Impacts of Changes in the Information Technology R&D Ecosystem*, The National Academies Press, Washington, D.C., p. 33, summarizing NRC/CSTB, 2003, *Innovation in Information Technology*, The National Academies Press, Washington, D.C., pp. 2-4.

biomedical computing; and the Intelligence Advanced Research Projects Activity invests in such areas as data analysis and speech translation.[17] Today, a wide array of agencies participate in the federal Networking and Information Technology Research and Development (NITRD) program,[18] reflecting their interest in supporting advances in various aspects of computing and communications to fulfill their missions.

Why has federal support been so effective in stimulating innovation in computing? As is discussed below, many factors have been important.

1. Federally funded programs have supported long-term research into fundamental aspects of computing, whose widespread practical benefits typically take years to realize.[19]

> **BOX 3**
> **Assessing the U.S. IT R&D Ecosystem**
>
> The U.S. information technology (IT) research and development (R&D) ecosystem was the envy of the world in 1995—from the perspective of IT, the United States enjoyed a strong industrial base, an ability to create and leverage ever newer technological advances, and an extraordinary system for creating world-class technology companies. But the period from 1995 to the present has been a turbulent one for the U.S. IT R&D ecosystem. Today, this ecosystem—encompassing university and industrial research enterprises, emerging start-up and more mature technology companies, those that finance innovative firms, and the regulatory environment and legal frameworks—remains unquestionably the strongest such ecosystem in the world.
>
> However, this position of leadership is not a birthright, and it has come under pressure. The IT industry has become more globalized, especially with the dramatic rise of the economies of India and China, fueled in no small part by their development of vibrant IT industries. Moreover, those nations represent fast-growing markets for IT products, and both are likely to build their IT industries into economic powerhouses for the world, reflecting deliberate government policies and the existence of strong, vibrant private-sector firms, both domestic and foreign. Ireland, Israel, Korea, Taiwan, Japan, and some Scandinavian countries have also developed strong niches within the increasingly globalized IT industry.
>
> As a result the United States risks ceding IT leadership to other nations within a generation unless it recommits to providing the resources needed to fuel U.S. IT innovation, to removing important roadblocks that reduce the ecosystem's effectiveness in generating innovation and the fruits of innovation, and to remaining a lead innovator and user of IT.
>
> SOURCE: Adapted from NRC/CSTB, 2009, *Assessing the Impacts of Changes in the Information Technology R&D Ecosystem*, The National Academies Press, Washington, D.C.

One of the most important messages of Figure 1 is the long, unpredictable incubation period—requiring steady work and funding—between initial exploration and commercial deployment.[20] The time from first concept to successful market is often measured in decades—a contrast to the more incremental innovations that tend to be publicized as evidence of the rapid pace of IT innovation. Starting a new project requires considerable time and often may be risky, but the payoffs can be enormous. It is often not clear which aspect of an early-stage research project will ultimately be the most important. Fundamental research produces a range of ideas, and those bringing technologies to market will draw on innovative ideas as needs emerge. Indeed, the utility of ideas may be evident only well after they have been generated. For example, early work in coding theory ultimately made possible the modern cell phone and streaming video over the Internet, and today's cloud computing owes much to decades of research in distributed computing.

Because of unanticipated results and synergies, the exact course of fundamental research cannot be planned in advance, and its progress cannot be measured precisely in the short term. Even projects that appear to have failed or whose results do not seem to have immediate utility often make significant contributions to later technology development or achieve other objectives not originally envisioned. The field of number theory provides a striking example. For hundreds of years a branch of pure mathematics without applications, it became a foundation for the public-key cryptography that underlies the security of electronic commerce.[21]

2. The interplay of government-funded academic research and industry R&D has been an important factor in IT commercialization.[22]

The examples in Figure 1 show the interplay between government-funded academic research and industry research and development. In some cases, such as reduced-instruction-set computing (RISC) processors that are widely used today in mobile phones and other low-power applications, the initial ideas came from industry, but the research that was essential to advancing these ideas came from government funding to universities. RISC was conceived at IBM (International Business Machines), but it was not commercialized until DARPA funded additional research at the University of California, Berkeley, and at Stanford University as part of its Very Large Scale Integrated Circuit (VLSI) program in the late 1970s and early 1980s.[23] RISC has since become commercially significant in a wide range of successful products from supercomputers to mobile phones. Of the 8.3 billion microprocessors produced in 2010, 6.1 billion implemented the Advanced RISC Machine (ARM) architecture.[24] The VLSI Design program also supported university research that gave rise to such companies as Cadence Design Systems, Synopsys, and Mentor Graphics, which acquired dozens of smaller companies that started as spin-offs of DARPA-funded[25] university research and today are part of a multibillion-dollar electronic design automation industry that is an essential enabler of other IT industries.

Similarly, although IBM pioneered the concept of relational databases (the System R project), it was NSF-sponsored research at the University of California, Berkeley, that brought this technology to a point at which it was commercialized by several start-up companies and then by more established database companies (including IBM).[26] Indeed, in none of the examples of products and industries shown in Figure 1 did industry alone provide the research necessary for success.

Moreover, these research-enabled commercial developments have expanded the possibilities for research, given that commercialization has led to substantial decreases in cost. Lower costs have allowed for much wider penetration of technology and have in turn greatly reduced the barrier for who gets to innovate, opening the door to a much wider range of both research and researchers, and to operation at a much larger scale, than was possible even 15 years ago.

3. There is a complex interweaving of fundamental research and focused development.[27]

The purpose of publicly funded research is to advance knowledge and to solve hard problems. The exploitation of that knowledge and those solutions in products is fundamentally important, but the form it takes is often unpredictable, as is the impact on future research (see the discussion of the technological underpinnings of e-commerce in Box 4). In the case of integrated circuit (VLSI) design tools, research innovation (at places like Stanford University, the University of California, Berkeley, and the University of North Carolina) led to products and then to major industrial markets. In the case of relational databases, research at the University of California, Berkeley, built on earlier work at IBM and led to the first commercialization of the technology. Later, the introduction of products stimulated new fundamental research questions, leading to a new generation of products with capabilities vastly greater than those of their predecessors. Another example is the theoretical research at the Massachusetts Institute of Technology that yielded the algorithms behind the technology for Web-content distribution networks, which provide the foundation for successful companies such as Akamai Technologies.

> **BOX 4**
> **The Research Underpinnings of Electronic Commerce—An Example**
>
> The most visible technology supporting e-commerce is the Word Wide Web, built on the Internet, which during the 1990s grew rapidly from a research network to critical societal infrastructure. Behind the Web interface lie a number of information technologies that have been developed incrementally over years or even decades and that have their roots in computing research. Important examples of such technologies include:
>
> - Distributed-computing technologies that support scaling up to very large numbers of users;
> - Approaches to facilitating data interchange, including mediator and wrapper techniques (which allow legacy systems to be integrated into newer systems) and the extensible markup language (XML) standard for describing data;
> - Safe mobile code capabilities, which enable code to be downloaded and run on end-user computing platforms;
> - Database/transaction capabilities, most notably the development of reliable, large-scale relational databases (and more recent object extensions); capabilities for ensuring integrity and consistency of databases; and the emergence of a standard language, structured query language (SQL), for querying databases;
> - Multimedia technologies, including techniques for compressing audio and video, which support streaming or downloaded content;
> - Graphical Web browsers, which made Internet services accessible to general users and across a wide range of hardware and software platforms;
> - Search engines, including indexing, query interfaces, and spiders that build indexes of Web content;
> - Data mining, which allows patterns to be inferred and relevant data to be identified from very large data sets;
> - Improved understanding of human-computer interface issues, ranging from page layout and navigation design to e-commerce transaction support and online collaboration;
> - Public-key and other cryptographic security capabilities that provide confidentiality and the integrity of in-transit and stored data, nonrepudiation of transactions, and the like; and
> - Other security capabilities, including authentication of users, network monitoring, and intrusion detection.
>
> ---
>
> SOURCE: Adapted from NRC/CSTB, 2002, *Information Technology Research, Innovation, and E-Government*, National Academy Press, Washington, D.C., p. 38.

4. Federal support for research has tended to complement, rather than preempt, industry investments in research.

The IT sector invests an enormous amount each year in R&D. It is critical to understand, however, that the vast majority of corporate R&D has always been focused on product and process development.[28] This is what shareholders (or other investors) demand. It is harder for corporations to justify funding long-term, fundamental research. Economists have articulated the concept of appropriability to express the extent to which the results of an investment can be captured by the investor, as opposed to being available to all players in the market. The results of long-term, fundamental research are hard to appropriate for several reasons: they tend to be published openly and thus to become generally known; they tend to have broad value; it is difficult to predict in advance which will be important; and they become known well ahead of the moment of realization as a product, and many parties thus have the opportunity to incorporate the results into their thinking. Such innovations effectively "raise everyone's boat" in the same way as do government investments in bioscience, health care, and other strategically important scientific disciplines.[29] In contrast, incremental research and product development can be performed in a way that is more appropriable. It can be done under wraps, and it can be moved into the marketplace more quickly and predictably.

Although individual industry players may find it hard to justify research that is weakly appropriable, it is the proper role of the federal government to support this sort of endeavor.[30] When companies create successful new products using the ideas and workforce that result from federally sponsored research, they repay the nation handsomely in jobs, tax revenues, productivity increases, and world leadership.[31] Long-term research often has great benefits for the IT sector as a whole, although no particular company can be sure of reaping most of these benefits. Appropriability also helps to explain why the companies that have tended to provide the greatest support for fundamental research are large companies that enjoy dominant positions in their market.[32]

Start-ups represent the other end of the spectrum. A hallmark of U.S. entrepreneurship, start-ups and start-up financing have facilitated the development of high-risk products as well as an iconoclastic, risk-taking attitude among more traditional companies and managers in the IT business. But they do not engage in research.[33] Thus, start-ups are notable for two reasons: first, although start-ups at least temporarily attract some researchers away from university-based research, they place them in a position to spearhead innovation, often based on their university work, and second, notwithstanding the popular labeling of start-ups as "high-tech," they apply the fruits of past research rather than generating more. In both respects, government funding plays a critical role in building the foundations for these innovative commercial investments.

UNIVERSITY RESEARCH AND BROADER ECONOMIC IMPACTS

Much of the government-funded research in IT has been carried out at universities.[34] Between 1976 and 2009 federal support constituted roughly two-thirds of total university research funding in computer science and electrical engineering.[35] Among the important characteristics of universities that contribute to their success as engines of innovation are the following:

- *Universities can focus on long-term research*, a special role of universities that IT companies cannot be expected to fill to the same extent.[36] (Universities' ability to carry out such research depends, of course, on federal and other sources of funding for research with a long time horizon.)
- *Universities provide a neutral ground for collaboration*, encouraging movement and interaction among faculty through leave and sabbatical policies that allow professors to visit industry, government, and other university departments or laboratories. Universities also provide sites at which researchers from competing companies can come together to explore technical issues.[37]
- *Universities integrate research and education*, a conjunction that creates very powerful synergies, ensuring that students are involved in projects where knowledge is being discovered, not only studied, and providing an educational foundation for the continuous learning that is so important in a fast-moving field like IT.[38]
- *Universities are inherently multidisciplinary*, and university researchers are well situated to draw on experts from a variety of fields.[39] Despite cultural barriers to cross-disciplinary

collaboration, physical proximity and collegial values go a long way in enabling collaboration. The multidisciplinary nature of universities is of historic and growing importance to computer science, which interfaces with so many other fields.
- *Universities are "open"* both literally and figuratively, a characteristic that can pay enormous unanticipated dividends. Chance interactions in an open environment can change the world; for example, when Microsoft founders Paul Allen and Bill Gates were students at Seattle's Lakeside School in the early 1970s, they were exposed to computing and computer science at the University of Washington and to a university spin-off company, Computer Center Corporation.

These characteristics of university research share a common element—people. U.S. research universities are unique in the degree to which they integrate research with education—in both undergraduate and graduate education. Universities educate the skilled IT workers of the future.[40] Their graduates are also by far the most effective vehicle for technology transfer, not only from universities to industry but also between university laboratories and departments, through the hiring of postdoctoral researchers and assistant professors.[41] Faculty and student researchers often move into product-development roles as consultants, employees, and entrepreneurs.[42] Federal support for university research drives this process. In Ph.D.-granting computer science programs, more than half of all graduate students receive financial support from the federal government, mostly in the form of research assistantships.[43]

Another benefit of federally funded academic research that doesn't show up in Figure 1 is research's contribution to the development of open standards and open-source codes that support further innovation. The standards that define the Internet had their origins in academic work, and federal support allowed many university researchers to participate in their development and evolution. The Hyper Text Transfer Protocol (HTTP) Daemon Web server developed with NSF support at the University of Illinois by the National Center for Supercomputing Applications powered much of the early Web, and its code base was used to develop the open-source Apache Web server that is widely used today. Similarly, many of the team members who developed the original Mosaic Web browser went on to commercialize the product in the form of Netscape Navigator. Moreover, the open-source Mozilla browser code became a foundation for the Firefox browser.

In addition to educating students and creating ideas and companies, universities often bring forefront technologies to their regions (e.g., the nationwide expansion of ARPANET in the 1970s and of NSFnet in the 1980s, and the continuation of those efforts through the private Internet activities in the 1990s and early 2000s), and universities serve as powerful magnets for companies seeking to relocate. Indeed, strong research institutions are recognized as being among the most critical success factors in high-tech economic development.[44,45]

Looking Ahead

Today's research investments are essential to tomorrow's world leadership in information technology (IT). Properly managed, publicly funded research in IT will continue to create important new technologies and industries, some of them unimagined today. Indeed, the field is young, and there is every reason to believe that the best is yet to come. Box 5 provides a few examples of the impacts that can be anticipated from advances in IT in the coming decades. Surely, however, some of the most important impacts will not have been listed, because—as history shows us—many of the technological surprises and major economic disruptions just waiting to happen cannot be predicted today.

The process of innovation will continue to take many years from the inception of a new idea to the creation of a billion-dollar industry. Every step of this process benefits from—and often requires—federal support. Without ongoing federal investment in fundamental research there would still be innovation, but the quantity and the range of new ideas for U.S. industry to draw from would be greatly diminished—as would the flow of people educated at the technological forefront, the most important product of the nation's research universities.[46]

The lessons of history are clear. A complex partnership among government, industry, and universities made the United States the world leader in IT, and information technology has become essential to our national security and economic and social well-being. The federal government's sponsorship of fundamental research in IT—largely university-based—has been and will continue to be essential.

> **BOX 5**
> **Examples of Advances Expected from Continued Commitment to Information Technology Research**
>
> - *Safer, robotics-enhanced automobiles.* The creation of a car that "cannot crash" has the potential to save tens of thousands of lives—and many more injuries—annually, while also giving U.S. products a competitive advantage in the automotive market.
> - *A more scalable, manageable, secure, and robust Internet.* Employing protocols that were developed nearly 40 years ago, today's Internet faces challenges in such areas as scalability, security, robustness, and manageability.
> - *Personalized and collaborative educational tools for tutoring and just-in-time learning.* Although information technology is not a cure-all, it does offer the potential to both enhance learning for all learners and transform the ways in which people learn. Such methods include adaptive tutors, collaborative authoring, learning in context and just-in-time learning, and flexible simulation.
> - *Personalized health monitoring.* Combined advances in processing power, microelectromechanical systems, sensors, and low-power radios are enabling an explosion of opportunities to create "sensors for everyone." Embedding these sensors in such devices as cellular telephones, wristwatches, and appliances can provide a great deal of important information about individuals' personal activity patterns which can be used to better advise patients on how to alter behavior.
> - *Augmented cognition to help people cope with information overload.* Although the wealth of information to which people are exposed continues to expand, their ability to absorb, evaluate, and act on it does not. IT contributes substantially to this overload, and it stands to reason that IT should also provide tools for assisting people in absorbing and evaluating information, and calling their attention to information that requires action.
> - *IT-driven advances in all fields of science and engineering.* A new form of computational science—focused on the collection of massive amounts of data from sensors around the world—has emerged. This development is aided by advances in techniques for storing, retrieving, mining, visualizing, and discovering knowledge in these data, and it has the potential to assist in discovering new information about everything from the inner workings of the body to events at the far reaches of the solar system.
>
> ---
>
> SOURCE: Adapted from NRC/CSTB, 2009, *Assessing the Impacts of Changes in the Information Technology R&D Ecosystem*, The National Academies Press, Washington, D.C., pp. 36-41.

Notes

MAIN TEXT

1. Section based on National Research Council (NRC)/Computer Science and Telecommunications Board (CSTB), 2009, *Assessing the Impacts of Changes in the Information Technology R&D Ecosystem: Retaining Leadership in an Increasingly Global Environment,* The National Academies Press, Washington, D.C., with additional data from the Bureau of Economic Analysis and the Networking and Information Technology Research and Development (NITRD) program.
2. NRC/CSTB, 2009, *Assessing the Impacts of Changes in the Information Technology R&D Ecosystem.*
3. As defined by the Department of Commerce, this industry cluster consists of "computer and electronic products within durable-goods manufacturing; publishing industries (includes software) and information and data processing services within information; and computer systems design and related services within professional, scientific, and technical services." See http://www.bea.gov/newsreleases/industry/gdpindustry/2011/txt/gdpind10_rev.
4. Bureau of Economic Analysis, 2011, "2010 Recovery Widespread Across Industries," April 26, http://www.bea.gov/newsreleases/industry/gdpindustry/2011/pdf/gdpind10_adv_fax.pdf. See also "Interactive Access to Industry Economic Accounts Data," http://www.bea.gov/iTable/iTable.cfm?ReqID=5&step=1.
5. Matthieu Pélissié du Rausas, James Manyika, Eric Hazan, Jacques Bughin, Michael Chui, and Rémi Said, 2011, "Internet Matters: The Net's Sweeping Impact on Growth, Jobs, and Prosperity," McKinsey Global Institute, May, http://www.mckinsey.com/Insights/MGI/Research/Technology_and_Innovation/Internet_matters. The authors define "Internet-related activities" as the "totality of Internet activities (e.g., e-commerce) and . . . a portion of the information and communication technologies sector delineated by such activities, technologies, and services linked to the Web."
6. This number may overestimate the investment in computing research. A 2010 PCAST report observes that "[a] large portion of the 'High End Computing Infrastructure and Applications' . . . is attributable to computational infrastructure used to conduct R&D in other fields." See President's Council of Advisors on Science and Technology, 2010, *Report to the President and Congress: Designing a Digital Future: Federally Funded Research and Development in Networking and Information Technology,* Executive Office of the President, http://www.whitehouse.gov/sites/default/files/microsites/ostp/pcast-nitrd-report-2010.pdf.
7. NITRD, 2009, "FY 2010 Networking and Information Technology Research and Development Supplement to the President's Budget," May, http://www.nitrd.gov/pubs/2010supplement/FY10Supp-FINALFormat-Web.pdf.

8. Section based on NRC/CSTB, 2003, *Innovation in Information Technology,* The National Academies Press, Washington, D.C., with discussion updated to take into account revisions reflected in Figure 1 of the present report.
9. NRC/CSTB, 1995, *Evolving the High Performance Computing and Communications Initiative to Support the Nation's Information Infrastructure,* National Academy Press, Washington, D.C.
10. NRC/CSTB, 2003, *Innovation in Information Technology.*
11. The idea that research in IT not only builds in part on research in physics, mathematics, electrical engineering, psychology, and other fields but also strongly influences them is consistent with what Donald Stokes has characterized in his four-part taxonomy as "Pasteur's Quadrant" research: use- or application-inspired basic research that pursues fundamental understanding (such as Louis Pasteur's research on the biological bases of fermentation and disease). See the discussion on pp. 26-29 of NRC/CSTB, 2000, *Making IT Better,* National Academy Press, Washington, D.C.; see also Donald E. Stokes, 1997, *Pasteur's Quadrant: Basic Science and Technological Innovation,* Brookings Institution Press, Washington, D.C.
12. NRC/CSTB, 2009, *Assessing the Impacts of Changes in the Information Technology R&D Ecosystem.*
13. NRC/CSTB, 1999, *Funding a Revolution: Government Support for Computing Research,* National Academy Press, Washington, D.C.
14. NRC/CSTB, 2009, *Assessing the Impacts of Changes in the Information Technology R&D Ecosystem.*
15. Some of the agencies within the Department of Defense that made major contributions include the Office of Naval Research, Air Force Office of Scientific Research, Army Research Office, and the Army's Satellite Communications Agency.
16. NRC/CSTB, 1999, *Funding a Revolution;* 1995, *Evolving the High Performance Computing and Communications Initiative to Support the Nation's Information Infrastructure.*
17. In addition to provision of research funding, complementary activities have been undertaken by other agencies, such as the National Institute of Standards and Technology, which often brings together people from universities and industry on issues relating to standards setting and measurement.
18. Member agencies include the Agency for Healthcare Research and Quality; Defense Advanced Research Projects Agency; Department of Homeland Security; Department of Energy—National Nuclear Security Administration and DOE Office of Advanced Scientific Computing Research; Environmental Protection Agency; Department of Health and Human Services—Office of the National Coordinator, National Archives and Records Administration; National Aeronautics and Space Administration; National Institutes of Health; National Institute of Standards and Technology; National Oceanic and Atmospheric Administration; National Security Agency; National Science Foundation; and Office of the Secretary of Defense and Department of Defense service research organizations (Defense Research and Engineering and Deputy Under Secretary of Defense Science & Technology). See http://www.nitrd.gov/Subcommittee/agency-web-sites.aspx.
19. NRC/CSTB, 1999, *Funding a Revolution.*
20. NRC/CSTB, 1999, *Funding a Revolution;* 1995, *Evolving the High Performance Computing and Communications Initiative to Support the Nation's Information Infrastructure.*
21. NRC/CSTB, 1999, *Funding a Revolution.*
22. See, for example, previous CSTB reports (all published by the National Academy/Academies Press, Washington, D.C.), including NRC/CSTB, 1999, *Funding a Revolution;* 2000, *Making IT Better;* 1995, *Evolving the High Performance Computing and Communications Initiative to Support the Nation's Information Infrastructure;* 1992, *Computing the Future: A Broader Agenda for Computer Science and Engineering;* 2001, *Building a Workforce for the Information Economy;* 1994, *Academic Careers in Experimental Computer Science and Engineering;* 2001, *Embedded, Everywhere: A Research Agenda for Networked Systems of Embedded Computers;* and 1997, *More Than Screen Deep: Toward Every-Citizen Interfaces to the Nation's Information Infrastructure.*
23. NRC/CSTB, 1999, *Funding a Revolution;* 1995, *Evolving the High Performance Computing and Communications Initiative to Support the Nation's Information Infrastructure.*
24. Timothy Prickett Morgan, 2011, "ARM Holdings Eager for PC and Server Expansion: Record 2010, Looking for Killer 2020," The Register Online, February 1, http://www.theregister.co.uk/2011/02/01/arm_holdings_q4_2010_numbers/.
25. In some cases, the Semiconductor Research Corporation provided the funding. For additional information, see http://web.archive.org/web/20080103002836/and http://www.src.org/member/about/history.asp.
26. NRC/CSTB, 1999, *Funding a Revolution;* 1995, *Evolving the High Performance Computing and Communications Initiative to Support the Nation's Information Infrastructure.*

27. See, for example, the following previous CSTB reports: NRC/CSTB, 1999, *Funding a Revolution*; 2000, *Making IT Better*; 1995, *Evolving the High Performance Computing and Communications Initiative to Support the Nation's Information Infrastructure*.
28. NRC/CSTB, 2000, *Making IT Better*.
29. NRC/CSTB, 2010, *Critical Code: Software Producibility for Defense*, The National Academies Press, Washington, D.C., p. 37.
30. NRC/CSTB, 1999, *Funding a Revolution*; 1995, *Evolving the High Performance Computing and Communications Initiative to Support the Nation's Information Infrastructure*.
31. NRC/CSTB, 1999, *Funding a Revolution*; 1995, *Evolving the High Performance Computing and Communications Initiative to Support the Nation's Information Infrastructure*.
32. NRC/CSTB, 1999, *Funding a Revolution*.
33. NRC/CSTB, 2000, *Making IT Better*.
34. The concentration of research in universities is particularly true for computer science research; industry played an important role in telecommunications research before the breakup of AT&T and the original Bell Labs. Important research has also been conducted at Department of Energy and other government laboratories.
35. NRC/CSTB, 2000, *Making IT Better*.
36. See, for example the following previous CSTB reports: NRC/CSTB, 1999, *Funding a Revolution*; 2000, *Making IT Better*; 1995, *Evolving the High Performance Computing and Communications Initiative to Support the Nation's Information Infrastructure*.
37. NRC/CSTB, 2000, *Making IT Better*; 1994, *Academic Careers in Experimental Computer Science and Engineering*.
38. NRC/CSTB, 2000, *Making IT Better*; 1992, *Computing the Future*.
39. NRC/CSTB, 2000, *Making IT Better*.
40. NRC/CSTB, 2001, *Building a Workforce for the Information Economy*.
41. NRC/CSTB, 2001, *Building a Workforce for the Information Economy*.
42. To the extent that U.S. research produces people who move to U.S. product development, the U.S. economy gains an "appropriable" benefit from funding research.
43. Computing Research Association (CRA), 2010, Taulbee Survey Report, CRA, Washington, D.C., Table 25, http://www.cra.org/resources/taulbee/.
44. NRC/CSTB, 2001, *Building a Workforce for the Information Economy*.
45. In computing, electronics, telecommunications, and biotechnology, evidence of the correlation abounds—in Boston (Harvard University and the Massachusetts Institute of Technology); Research Triangle Park (Duke University, the University of North Carolina, and North Carolina State University); New Jersey (Princeton University, Rutgers University, and New York City–based Columbia University); Austin (the University of Texas); southern California (the University of California, San Diego, the University of California, Los Angeles, the California Institute of Technology, and the University of Southern California); northern California (the University of California, Berkeley, the University of California, San Francisco, and Stanford University); and Seattle (the University of Washington).
46. See, for example, previous CSTB reports, including NRC/CSTB, 1999, *Funding a Revolution*; 2000, *Making IT Better*; 1995, *Evolving the High Performance Computing and Communications Initiative to Support the Nation's Information Infrastructure*; 1992, *Computing the Future*; 2001, *Building a Workforce for the Information Economy*; 1994, *Academic Careers in Experimental Computer Science and Engineering*; 2001, *Embedded, Everywhere*; and 1997, *More Than Screen Deep*.

TABLE 1

Qualcomm—Equipment and services ($6.98 billion); licensing and royalties ($4.01 billion). Qualcomm 2010 Annual Report, http://files.shareholder.com/downloads/QCOM/1510480689x0x451979/c5ba4b26-fe1d-4756-a735-ed1d972402cb/2010-10-K.pdf.

Motorola—Net sales, products ($6.1 billion); net sales, services ($2.1 billion). Motorola 2011 Annual Report, http://files.shareholder.com/downloads/ABEA-2FO3VV/1751114768x0x552627/1344EB61-45BA-4EAD-9EC4-A99116BE997C/MSI_2011_AR.pdf.

nVidia—FY2011 total revenue. nVidia Corporation, 2011 Annual Review, Notice of Annual Meeting, Proxy Statement and nVidia Form 10-K (U.S. Securities and Exchange Commission; SEC).

Intel—2011 revenue based on general accepted accounting principles (GAAP); non-GAAP revenue $54.2 billion. See http://www.intc.com/financials.cfm.

AMD—Computing solutions only (excludes "graphics," "foundries," and "other"). AMD 2011 Annual Report, http://ir.amd.com/phoenix.zhtml?c=74093&p=irol-reportsannual.

Texas Instruments—2011 revenue from embedded processing segment, http://files.shareholder.com/downloads/TXN/1710273597x0x535657/2de80eb4-2af1-4e4e-bd7f-f36811701b17/TXN_News_2012_1_23_Financial.pdf.

Dell—Desktop PCs ($18.97 billion) and mobile and laptop PCs ($14.69 billion) (excludes software, services, and enterprise/server sales). Dell 2011 Form 10-K (SEC).

HP—Revenue from Personal Systems Group (excludes software, services, and printers). HP 2011 Annual Report, http://h30261.www3.hp.com/phoenix.zhtml?c=71087&p=irol-reportsAnnual.

Apple—Includes desktop and portable device sales ($21.78 billion), iPhone ($47.0 billion), and iPad ($20.3 billion). 2011 Apple, Inc. Form 10-K (SEC).

Symantec—Symantec FY2011 net revenue, http://phx.corporate-ir.net/External.File?item=UGFyZW50SUQ9NDQ2MTY2fENoaWxkSUQ9NDY5NTEwfFR5cGU9MQ==&t=1.

Juniper—Total revenue. Juniper Networks FY2011 Form 10-K (SEC).

Cisco—Total revenue. Cisco Systems 2011 Annual Report, http://www.cisco.com/assets/cdc_content_elements/docs/annualreports/media/2011-ar.pdf.

Akamai—Total revenue. Akamai FY2011 Form 10-K (SEC).

Twitter—Estimated total revenue. *Wall Street Journal*, 2011, "Twitter as Tech Bubble Barometer," http://www.npr.org/blogs/thetwo-way/2011/02/10/133648669/twitters-value-up-to-10-billion-wall-street-journal-reports.

Facebook—Total 2011 revenue. Form 424B4 (SEC), filed May 18, 2012.

eBay—Total revenue. eBay FY2011 Form 10-K (SEC).

Amazon—Sum of U.S.-based media sales ($8 billion) and electronics and merchandise sales ($17.3 billion); excludes Amazon Web Services and "other," which encompasses such things as Amazon-branded credit cards. Amazon FY2011 Form 10-K (SEC).

Google—Revenue except "other." Google FY2010 Form 10-K (SEC).

Yahoo!—Total FY2011 revenue. Yahoo! FY2011 Form 10-K (SEC).

Google—Non-advertising revenue. Google FY2010 Form 10-K (SEC).

VMware—Total revenue. VMware FY2010 Form 10-K (SEC).

Amazon—Non-e-commerce revenue from Amazon Web Services. Amazon FY2011 Form 10-K (SEC).

Oracle—Revenue total for new software licenses ($9.2 billion), hardware systems ($4.4 billion), software license updates and product support ($14.8 billion), and hardware systems support ($2.56 billion) and excluding cloud, consulting, and education. Oracle FY2010 Form 10-K (SEC).

IBM—2011 revenue from software ($24.94 billion) and systems and technology ($18.99 billion) and excluding global business services, global technology services, and global financing. IBM 2011 Annual Report, http://www.ibm.com/annualreport/2011/.

Microsoft—Revenue from server and tools product and service offerings (includes Windows Server, Microsoft SQL Server, Windows Azure, Visual Studio, System Center products, Windows Embedded device platforms, and Enterprise Services) ($17.1 billion); Business Division offerings (includes the Microsoft Office system, comprising mainly Office, SharePoint, Exchange, and Lync; and Microsoft Dynamics business solutions) ($22.2 billion). Microsoft FY2011 Form 10-K (SEC).

Electronic Arts—Electronic Arts FY2010 Form 10-K (SEC).

Pixar—Pixar became a wholly owned subsidiary of the Walt Disney Company in 2006. Worldwide gross revenue from Pixar Studio releases was $766 million in 2009, $1.06 billion in 2010, and $554 million in 2011. See http://www.the-numbers.com/movies/series/Pixar.php.

Adobe—Total revenue. Adobe FY2011 Form 10-K (SEC).

iRobot—Total revenue. iRobot 2010 Annual Report, April 13, 2011, http://phx.corporate-ir.net/External.File?item=UGFyZW50SUQ9NDIxNzg2fENoaWxkSUQ9NDM1NTYzfFR5cGU9MQ==&t=1.

Nuance—Total revenue. Nuance FY2011 Form 10-K (SEC).

Intuitive Surgical—Total revenue. Intuitive Surgical 2010 Annual Report, http://phx.corporate-ir.net/External.File?item=UGFyZW50SUQ9ODQxMTJ8Q2hpbGRJRD0tMXxUeXBlPTM=&t=1.

TABLE 2

Column Headed "Today"

Wireless and broadband industry

subscribers worldwide: International Telecommunication Union, 2011, "The World in 2011: ICT Facts and Figures," http://www.itu.int/ITU-D/ict/facts/2011/material/ICTFactsFigures2010.pdf.

subscribers in the United States: CTIA, "50 Wireless Quick Facts," http://www.ctia.org/consumer_info/index.cfm/AID/10323.

mobile-broadband subscribers: International Telecommunication Union, 2011, "Measuring the Information Society," http://www.itu.int/ITU-D/ict/publications/idi/2011/Material/MIS_2011_without_annex_5.pdf.

fixed broadband subscriptions: Organisation for Economic Cooperation and Development, Directorate for Science, Technology, and Industry, "OECD Broadband Portal," http://www.oecd.org/document/54/0,3746,en_2649_34225_38690102_1_1_1_1,00.html.

Microprocessor industry

8.3 billion: Lee Eng Kean, 2010, "MCU to Intel Architecture Conversion," *EE Times*, May 31, http://www.eetimes.com/design/microcontroller-mcu/4199788/MCU-to-Intel-architecture-conversion.

$40 billion: http://www.isuppli.com/Home-and-Consumer-Electronics/News/Pages/Fourth-Quarter-2010-Microprocessor-Shares–Final-Microprocessor-Revenue-Share-Data.aspx.

Personal computing industry

1.4 billion: eTForecasts, "Worldwide PC Market," http://www.etforecasts.com/products/ES_pcww1203.htm.

100 million: "Gartner Survey Shows U.S. Consumers More Likely to Purchase a Smartphone Than Other Consumer Devices in 2011," http://www.gartner.com/it/page.jsp?id=1550814.

Internet and Web industries

One third . . . online, and 45%: International Telecommunication Union, 2011, "The World in 2011: ICT Facts and Figures," http://www.itu.int/ITU-D/ict/facts/2011/material/ICTFactsFigures2010.pdf.

18 billion searches: comScore, 2011, "comScore Releases 2011 U.S. Search Engine Rankings," press release, November 11, http://www.comscore.com/Press_Events/Press_Releases/2011/11/comScore_Releases_October_2011_U.S._Search_Engine_Rankings.

$48.2 billion and . . . 4.6% of total sales: U.S. Census Bureau, 2011, "Quarterly Retail E-Commerce Sales: 3rd Quarter 2011," November 17, http://www.fortune3.com/blog/2011/01/ecommerce-sales-2011/.

$8 trillion: Matthieu Pélissié du Rausas, James Manyika, Eric Hazan, Jacques Bughin, Michael Chui, and Rémi Said, 2011, "Internet Matters: The Net's Sweeping Impact on Growth, Jobs, and Prosperity," McKinsey Global Institute, May, http://www.mckinsey.com/Insights/MGI/Research/Technology_and_Innovation/Internet_matters.

Cloud computing industry

$1 billion . . . by 2013: In Stat, 2011, "Healthcare to Spend $518 Million on Infrastructure as a Service in 2015," August 1, http://www.instat.com/newmk.asp?ID=3219&SourceID=00000352000000000000.

Expand 139% from 2010 to 2011: Business Technology Roundtable, 2011, "Increased Spending on Public Cloud Computing Services," August 9, http://business-technology-roundtable.blogspot.com/2011/08/increased-spending-on-public-cloud.html.

Enterprise systems industry

583 terabytes of sales: Information Week, 2006, "Data, Data Everywhere," http://www.informationweek.com/news/175801775?pgno=2; Regis McKenna, 2002, *Total Access: Giving Customers What They Want in an Anytime Anywhere World*, Harvard Business Press.

Entertainment industry

Highest-grossing film of 2010: Box Office Mojo, "2010 Worldwide Grosses," http://boxofficemojo.com/yearly/chart/?view2=worldwide&yr=2010&p=.htm.

Column Headed "Advances Expected," in Research Topic Noted

Networking

embedded everywhere: NRC/CSTB, 2001, *Embedded, Everywhere: A Research Agenda for Networked Systems of Embedded Computers*, National Academy Press, Washington. D.C.

Databases

energy-efficient computing: Stavros Harizopoulos, Mehul Shah, Justin Mexa, and Parthasarathy Ranganathan, 2009, "Energy Efficiency: The New Holy Grail of Data Management Systems Research," 4th Biennial Conference on Innovative Data Systems Research (CIDR), January 4-7, Asilomar, California.

and other large-scale data management systems: Daniel J. Abadi, 2009, "Data Management in the Cloud: Limitations and Opportunities," *Bulletin of the [IEEE Computer Society] Technical Committee on Data Engineering* 32(1):3-12; Sam Madden and Maarten van Steen, 2012, "Internet-Scale Data Management," *IEEE Internet Computing* 16(1):10-12.

Computer graphics

to the simulation code: James Ahrens and Han-Wei Shen, 2010, "Ultrascale Visualization," *IEEE Computer Graphics and Applications* 30(3):20-21.

Artificial intelligence and robotics

robots for more than vacuuming: Hans Moravec, 2009, "Rise of the Robots—The Future of Artificial Intelligence," *Scientific American*, March 23, http://www.scientificamerican.com/article.cfm?id=rise-of-the-robots.

Appendix A

Short Biographies of Committee Members

Peter Lee (*Chair*) is a corporate vice president of Microsoft Research in Redmond, Washington. Prior to taking his position at Microsoft, Dr. Lee worked at the Defense Advanced Research Projects Agency (DARPA), where he was the founding director of the Transformational Convergence Technology Office. Prior to DARPA, Dr. Lee was a professor and the head of the Computer Science Department at Carnegie Mellon University. Peter Lee's research contributions are in areas related to the foundations of software reliability, program analysis, security, and language design. A fellow of the Association for Computing Machinery and former chair of the board of directors of the Computing Research Association, Peter Lee is called on in diverse venues as a contributor in research, education, and policy making. He conducted his doctoral studies at the University of Michigan.

Mark E. Dean is chief technology officer, IBM Middle East and Africa. He was previously a technical fellow and vice president, worldwide operations at IBM Research, and the vice president for Systems Research at IBM's Watson Research Center in Yorktown Heights, New York, where he was responsible for the research and application of systems technologies spanning circuits to operating environments. During his career, Dr. Dean has held several engineering positions at IBM in the area of computer system hardware architecture and design. He has developed all types of computer systems, from embedded systems to supercomputers, including testing of the first gigahertz CMOS microprocessor, and he established the team that developed the Blue Gene supercomputer. He was also chief engineer for the development of the IBM PC/AT, ISA systems bus, PS/2 Model 70 and 80, and the color graphics adapter in the original IBM PC, and he holds three of the nine patents for the original IBM PC. One invention—the Industry Standard Architecture (ISA) "bus," which permitted add-on devices like the keyboard, disk drives, and printers to be connected to the motherboard—earned election to the National Inventors Hall of Fame for Dean and colleague Dennis Moeller. Dr. Dean's most recent awards include a National Institute of Science Outstanding Scientist Award, member of the American Academy of Arts and Sciences and the National Academy of Engineering, IEEE Fellow, the CCG Black Engineer of the Year, the NSBE Distinguished Engineer Award, the University of Tennessee COE Dougherty Award, and recipient of the Ronald H.

Brown American Innovators Award. Dr. Dean was appointed an IBM Fellow in 1995, IBM's highest technical honor. He is a member of the IBM Academy of Technology. Dr. Dean has more than 40 patents or patents pending. He received a BSEE degree from the University of Tennessee in 1979, an MSEE degree from Florida Atlantic University in 1982, and a Ph.D. in electrical engineering from Stanford University in 1992.

Deborah L. Estrin is a professor of computer science at UCLA and is director of the NSF-funded Center for Embedded Networked Sensing (CENS). Professor Estrin received her Ph.D. (1985) in computer science from the Massachusetts Institute of Technology, her M.S. (1982) from MIT, and her B.S. (1980) from the University of California, Berkeley. Before joining UCLA she was a member of the University of Southern California Computer Science Department from 1986 through the middle of 2000. In 1987, Professor Estrin received the National Science Foundation's Presidential Young Investigator Award for her research in network interconnection and security. During the subsequent 10 years much of her research focused on the design of network and routing protocols for very large, global networks, self-configuring protocol mechanisms for scalability and robustness, and tools and methods for designing and studying large-scale networks. Since the late 1990s Professor Estrin has been collaborating with her colleagues and students to develop protocols and systems architectures needed to realize rapidly deployable and robustly operating networks of many hundreds of physically embedded devices, e.g., sensor networks. She is particularly interested in the application of spatially and temporally dense embedded sensors to environmental monitoring. Dr. Estrin has been a co-principal investigator on many NSF- and DARPA-funded projects. She chaired a 1997-1998 ISAT study on sensor networks and the 2001 NRC study on networked embedded computing which produced the report *Embedded, Everywhere*. Professor Estrin serves on the advisory committees for the NSF Computer and Information Science and Engineering (CISE) and Environmental Research and Education (ERE) Directorates. She is a fellow of the ACM, AAAS, and IEEE. She has served on numerous panels for the NSF, National Academy of Sciences/NRC, and DARPA. She has also served as an editor for the ACM/IEEE *Transactions on Networks* and as a program committee member for many networking-related conferences, including Sigcomm and Infocom. She was general co-chair for the first ACM Conference on Embedded Networked Sensor Systems, SenSys 2003. She was also an associate editor for the new ACM *Transactions on Sensor Networks* and was a member of the National Research Council's Computer Science and Telecommunications Board from 2004 to 2011.

James T. Kajiya is currently a director of research at Microsoft Corporation. From 1994 to 1997, Dr. Kajiya was a senior researcher at Microsoft Research, where he built and led the graphics group. His recent work has focused on very-high-quality computer graphics. Most recently, Dr. Kajiya has returned to graphics hardware design. He was the principal architect on Talisman, a low-cost hardware architecture for very-high-quality real-time three-dimensional graphics. Dr. Kajiya also served as the principal investigator on a joint research project with IBM that produced an implementation of Prolog yielding a speed of 0.9 megalips and a new object-oriented systems programming language called FITH. In other work, he explored parallel ray tracing on the IBM RP3 and specified software architecture for scientific visualization in the IBM SVS, which became the Power Visualization System. In joint work with TRW, he has served as architect for supercomputers oriented toward military signal- and image-processing tasks. Dr. Kajiya has served on the external advisory board of the Defense Mapping Agency, on the National Neurocircuitry Database Committee for the National Academy of Sciences and Institute of Medicine, and on the

SIGGRAPH executive committee. He received the SIGGRAPH Technical Achievement Award in 1991 and served as the technical program chair for SIGGRAPH 93. In 1997, Dr. Kajiya, along with Dr. Timothy Kay, received an Academy Award (technical certificate) for work on rendering hair and fur. In 2002 he was elected to the National Academy of Engineering for contributions to formal and practical methods of computer image generation. He received a Ph.D. in computer science from the University of Utah.

Prabhakar Raghavan is vice president of engineering at Google, Inc. He is also a consulting professor of computer science at Stanford University. His research interests include text and Web mining and algorithm design, and he has authored two textbooks on the subjects. Dr. Raghavan received his Ph.D. from the University of California, Berkeley, and is a member of the National Academy of Engineering and a fellow of the ACM and the IEEE. Prior to joining Google he was head of Yahoo! Labs and before that, senior vice-president and chief technology officer at Verity; before that he held a number of technical and managerial positions at IBM Research.

Andrew J. Viterbi is a co-founder and retired vice chair and chief technical officer of QUALCOMM Incorporated. He spent equal portions of his career in industry, having previously co-founded Linkabit Corporation, and in academia as a professor in the Schools of Engineering and Applied Science, first at UCLA and then at UCSD, at which he is now a professor emeritus. He is currently president of the Viterbi Group, a technical advisory and investment company. He also serves as Presidential Chair Visiting Professor at the University of Southern California and as a distinguished visiting professor at the Technion-Israel Institute of Technology. Dr. Viterbi has received numerous honors both in the United States and internationally. Among these are seven honorary doctorates, from universities in Canada, Israel, Italy, and the United States; the Marconi International Fellowship Award; the IEEE Alexander Graham Bell, the Claude Shannon, and the James Clerk Maxwell Awards; the NEC C&C Award; the Eduard Rhein Foundation Award; the Christopher Columbus Medal, the Franklin Medal, and the Robert Noyes Semiconductor Industry Award; the Millennium Laureate Award; and the IEEE's highest award, the Medal of Honor. He is a member of the National Academy of Engineering and the National Academy of Sciences and is a fellow of the American Academy of Arts and Sciences. He has received an honorary title from the president of Italy and the National Medal of Science from the president of the United States. Dr. Viterbi serves on boards and committees of numerous nonprofit institutions, including the University of Southern California, MIT (Visiting Committee for Bioengineering), Mathematical Sciences Research Institute, Burnham Institute for Medical Research, and Scripps Translational Science Institute, and he is the past chair of the Computer and Information Sciences Section of the National Academy of Sciences.

Appendix B

Transfers of Ideas and People and Other Impacts Since 2003 Added to Figure 1

Table B.1 gives some examples of the many transfers of ideas and people and other impacts that occurred as the fields of computing and communications progressed, and it provides annotation for events depicted by arrows in Figure 1. It is not meant to be a comprehensive description of the history of the research in any of the areas listed.

TABLE B.1 Transfers and Other Impacts Since 2003 as Indicated by the New Arrows Added to Figure 1

Research Track and Events	Origins	Impact
Digital Communications		
Multiple-input and multiple-output	Closely related university research pre-1996; industry R&D (Bell Labs BLAST) in 1998	A fundamental enabler in today's wireless communications, including WiFi, WiMax, 4G, LTE, and others
Radio-frequency complementary metal-oxide semiconductor integrated circuits	Basic research and some serious engineering efforts in universities throughout the 1990s	The foundational device technology for WiFi, GPS, Bluetooth, and others
Wireless locating	Industry R&D in the early 2000s, with subsequent university research	Fundamental to some wireless systems, and an energy-saving supplement to GPS for mobile devices; now a foundation for growing location-based services
Bluetooth	Ericsson and open SIG 1994, with participation by industry and university; based on earlier research in spread-spectrum radio	Now the industry standard for very-short-range secure networking; used primarily for local connectivity of devices
MACA channel access protocol	University and industry research starting in 1990 and continuing to 2000s	The foundation for collision avoidance on shared physical network links, particularly for wireless networks
Computer Architecture		
Adaptive branch predictors	Two-level adaptive branch predictors started in academic research around 1992	Significant influence on subsequent research, as well as influence on modern processor designs
Memory-dependence predictors	Both university and industrial research, emerging in practical form around 1996-1997	Fundamental to enabling aggressive out-of-order execution in practice, affecting research in compilers and architectures, and commercial products
Multicore	Early university-based developments, such as Stanford Hydra and MIT RAW, circa 2002; later, industry R&D such as Sun's Niagara, around 2005	Fundamental to all processor architectures on the market today; furthermore, the problems of parallel computing have become central in research
Stream-based image-processing architectures	University-based research on stream-processing for image and signal processing, leading to developments such as Imagine, circa 2002	The foundation for today's GPUs; today there is considerable research and commercial development on applications that go far beyond graphics processing
Graphical processing unit in iPhone	Industry 2007	Present in mobile computers for some time, now considered de rigueur, given the user-experience advantages demonstrated by the iPad/iPhone
Advances in parallel computing applied to commercial product development	Continued university work on parallel computing in 2000s and earlier	Collaboration by top computer architecture researchers in academia and movement between the university and industry communities

TABLE B.1 Continued

Research Track and Events	Origins	Impact
Software Technologies		
Modern virtual machines	A long history of university research, with recent practical developments such as DISCO in 1997, and companies like VMware in 1998	A fundamental building block of cloud technology, allowing more effective provisioning of data-center services and security
Modern buffer overrun protections	Universities and industry throughout the 2000s	Operating systems starting to incorporate dynamic methods for improving security
Web 2.0	Industry, 2004	A fundamental shift in thinking in the operating system research community, as a new layer of distributed application infrastructure emerges
Multitouch appears in iPhone	Industry, 2007	New research thrusts in gesture-based user interfaces and some re-thinking of system architectures
Kinect	Industry, 2010	Originally designed as a game controller, then adopted by researchers as a new core sensor for many applications
Networking		
Content distribution networks	Early foundations developed in universities, contributing algorithms, systems concepts, and people to companies such as Akamai, 1998	A fundamental part of how the Internet works, essential to provision of services such as YouTube, news sites, and many others
Multiprotocol label switching	Early developments in companies such as Ipsilon Networks, circa 1996	Had a fundamental influence on subsequent university research in networking
GigaScope and others	Industry and university research, in particular AT&T Labs around 2003	Stream-based measurement and traffic analysis on large networks (and the Internet)—a fundamental tool for today's research
OpenFlow	Stanford University, 2008	Issued as a standard in 2011
Parallel and Distributed Systems		
Map-Reduce	Fundamental ideas date back to the 1960s, but made practical at scale by Google in 2004	Changed the research thinking in distributed computing; a foundation for many cloud systems
Hadoop	Open-source development, around 2006	Had immediate influence on university research, including not only distributed systems but also areas such as machine learning and databases; increasingly the base for commercial offerings
Message passing interface	A university and industry standards development, around 1994	The standard mechanism for programming high-performance computers

continued

TABLE B.1 Continued

Research Track and Events	Origins	Impact
Parallel and Distributed Systems (continued)		
Parallel virtual machine	Originated at Oakridge National Laboratory and university around 1990-1991	A key foundation for programming a networked collection of computers as a single system, for both research and practical applications
Peer-to-peer	Open community, picking up steam around 2004	Significant influence on a wide variety of widely used systems, such as Skype
Databases		
Researchers leave Stanford to found Google	University to start-up, 1998	Google
Data integration technologies	University and industry R&D throughout the 2000s	Fundamental impact on the "big data" movement, as seen in technologies such as Google Fusion Tables (2009)
Data-stream management systems	Industry R&D in the early 2000s	A key driver and enabler for both research and commercial developments in "big data"
XML	Broad community process in 1997; earlier SGML late 1980s	A key foundation for representation of online content on the Web and other IT-based systems
Computer Graphics		
Poisson image editing	Industry R&D, 2003	A major advance in image editing, now a core of image-processing tools (like Photoshop) and associated algorithms
Image stitching	Industry and university research, circa 2005	Omnipresent, from its use in mapping services (e.g., Google Maps) to modern filmmaking and panorama features in cameras
Spherical harmonic shading	Universities, around 2002	A major advance in (relatively) low-overhead realistic shading and shadowing in computer graphics
LightStage real-time capture	Universities (especially University of Southern California), in 2002	A foundation for today's digital image capture, used widely with particular impact in moviemaking and recognized recently with an Academy Award
Stable fluids and related methods	Universities, around 1999	The core of all image and video rendering for realistic smoke, water, and so on
Disney/Pixar labs	Industry-university partnership, in 2007	Similar to the Intel "lablet" model, for closer collaboration between industry and university research

TABLE B.1 Continued

Research Track and Events	Origins	Impact
AI and Robotics		
Incremental heuristic search	Universities, around 2004	A building block for a wide array of data mining and search technologies, as well as a foundation for basic research
Hidden Markov models for biology, speech, and the like	University and industry R&D throughout the 1990s	A major step in the general reduction of problems outside of core computing (genomics, speech processing, and so on) to algorithmic problems
Recommender systems	University and industry R&D, circa 1994	A core element of today's e-commerce systems
Bayesian methods applied	University and industry R&D throughout the 1990s	Fundamental to the major shift toward more statistical approaches to machine intelligence
Kinect audio and vision	Microsoft, 2010	The most rapidly adopted consumer electronics device of all time

Appendix C

Examples of Impacts from Algorithms Research

Research in theory and algorithms (see Box 1, "Research in the Theoretical and Algorithmic Foundations of Computing") has provided an important foundation for the advances depicted in Figure 1. Shown in Table C.1 are some of the many examples of research advances in algorithms that have helped lead to substantial economic impact.

TABLE C.1 Algorithms Research—Some Examples of Impacts

Research Topic	Origins	Impact
Algorithms for network congestion	Universities in the mid-1990s	A key building block for today's networking technologies, such as content-distribution networks
CPLEX	Universities pre-1985, later work in industry and start-ups (e.g., ILOG, IBM, and others)	A foundation for a wide array of practical optimization and resource-allocation problems and for logistics, delivery systems, and so on
Turbo codes	Decades of university and industry research, reduced to practical form at Telecom-Bretagne in 1993	Absolutely essential in digital communications, and in particular in wireless networking technologies today
Eigenvalues, PageRank, and so on	Decades of university research; PageRank emerged out of Stanford in 1998	PageRank the core of Google search; today, related concepts still fundamental
Distributed hash tables	Universities and industry, with practical algorithms available by 2001	A core element of today's peer-to-peer systems; also a strong influence on university and industry R&D
VCG auction mechanism	University research, emerging in 2000	A major impact on online advertising in the major search engines
N-gram matching for natural language processing	University and industry research, emerging as practical around 2004	The core of today's language-processing and translation systems